# ED SHEERAN

### BY JILL SHERMAN

AMICUS LEARNING

**Inspire is published by**
**Amicus Learning, an imprint of Amicus**
P.O. Box 227
Mankato, MN 56002
www.amicuspublishing.us



**Editor:** Ana Brauer
**Series Designer:** Kathleen Petelinsek
**Book Designer and Photo Researcher:** Emily Dietz

**Library of Congress Cataloging-in-Publication Data**
Names: Sherman, Jill, author.
Title: Ed Sheeran / by Jill Sherman.
Description: Mankato, MN : Amicus Learning, 2025. | Series: Inspire | Includes bibliographical
   references and index. | Audience: Ages 5–9 | Audience: Grades 2–3 | Summary: "Learn about British
   musician Ed Sheeran and his accomplishments in this biography packed with photos and fact-filled
   text suitable for young readers. Includes a table of contents, glossary, further resources, and index"
   —Provided by publisher.
Identifiers: LCCN 2024012075 (print) | LCCN 2024012076 (ebook) | ISBN 9798892001045 (library
   binding) | ISBN 9798892001625 (paperback) | ISBN 9798892002202 (ebook)
Subjects: LCSH: Sheeran, Ed, 1991—Juvenile literature. | Singers—England—Biography—
   Juvenile literature.
Classification: LCC ML3930.S484 S54 2025  (print) | LCC ML3930.S484  (ebook) |
   DDC 782.42164092 [B]—dc23/eng/20240315
LC record available at https://lccn.loc.gov/2024012075
LC ebook record available at https://lccn.loc.gov/2024012076

**Photo Credits:** Alamy Stock Photo/Matt Crossick, cover; Associated Press/Charles
Sykes, 2, Liam McBurney, 15; Getty Images/Chris Jackson, 16–17, Gareth Cattermole/
TAS, 12, Heritage Images, 7, JMEnternational, 18, Joe Maher/Disasters Emergency
Committee, 4, Michael Kovac, 11, PYMCA/Avalon, 8, Rebecca Sapp, 14, Total
Guitar Magazine, 10; Shutterstock/Selyutina Olga, 13

# Table of Contents

Fans of Ed Sheeran call themselves Sheerios.
Sheeran
LOOPER

# The A Team

Ed Sheeran first played his song "The A Team" at open mics and R&B clubs in 2009. Today, he plays the hit song on a stage for thousands of fans. Sheeran went from a kid from Suffolk, England to becoming one of the most famous British musicians today.

# Starting Out

Music came easily to Sheeran. He began singing in a church choir when he was four. He was 11 years old when he picked up his first guitar. It was a gift from his uncle. Sheeran quickly learned a few chords. Right away, he started writing his own songs.



**PLAY IT AGAIN!**
The first song Sheeran learned to play was "Layla" by Eric Clapton.

Sheeran's song "Castle on the Hill"
is based on a castle in England
near where he grew up.

At the start of his career, Sheeran performed at different theaters around London.

# Big Moves

Sheeran dreamed of being a musician. At 17, he quit school. He moved from Suffolk to London in 2008. He started playing **gigs** anywhere he could. He played at bars and empty restaurants. But that wasn't going to get him noticed by a record label. Sheeran needed to do something big.

# California Dreamin'

Sheeran's next stop on the road to stardom? Hollywood! He stayed with friends. He played more gigs. His talent shined. In 2010, American actor Jamie Foxx noticed him. Foxx invited Sheeran to use his **recording studio**.

**NICKNAMES**
Sheeran names his guitars. They have names like James, Trevor, and Keith.

Sheeran became famous in America shortly after he was discovered by actor Jamie Foxx.

Sheeran appeared on
stage with Taylor Swift
during her tour in 2014.

# Friends in High Places

Doors started opening for Sheeran. In 2011, he signed a record deal. The company was Elton John's! Then Sheeran was invited to go on tour. He would be the opening act. Who was the artist? Taylor Swift!

**DOUBLE ACT**
Sheeran and Swift became friends and released songs together. Their first song was "Everything Has Changed" on Swift's album, *Red*.

# Mathematical

Sheeran's albums have interesting names. The titles are math symbols. They have special meanings for Sheeran. His album, *X (Multiply)*, took everything from *+ (Plus)* and made it bigger.

**AWARD WINNER**

Sheeran won his first Grammy Award with X. As of 2024, he has won four Grammys.

In 2022, Sheeran began
his Mathematics world tour.
It was named after his albums.

Sheeran adds his handprint to a mural at a fundraiser to support people with lung cancer.

# Giving Back

Sheeran knows how hard it is to be a musician. Starting out is hard. That's why he started the Ed Sheeran Suffolk Music **Foundation** (ESSMF). It provides young musicians with money for lessons or new instruments.

Sheeran and his wife
first met as kids. They
reconnected in 2015.

# Family Man

Do you like love songs? So does Sheeran. He wrote the song "Perfect" about his girlfriend, Cherry Seaborn. How romantic! The couple married in 2019. They have two daughters.

# The Sky's the Limit

Ed Sheeran loves his job. He is always writing new songs. His music blends many **genres**. You can hear folk, rock, R&B, pop, and hip-hop in his music. What will his next album sound like? We'll have to wait and see!

Sheeran finished his Mathematics world tour in 2024, and he has plans to write a new album.

### ED SHEERAN

**Birthday:** February 17, 1991

**Hometown:** Framlingham, Suffolk, England

**Children:** 2

### AWARDS THROUGH 2024

**Billboard Music Awards:** 8

**Emmy Awards:** 1

**Grammys:** 4

**Kids' Choice Awards:** 2

### ALBUMS

+ (2011)

× (2014)

÷ (2017)

*No. 6 Collaborations Project* (2019)

= (2021)

− (2023)

*Autumn Variations* (2023)

# GLOSSARY

**chord**  A group of music notes played at the same time.

**foundation**  An organization that gives gifts of money to individuals or groups in need.

**genre**  A particular type or style of music.

**gig**  A live performance of music.

**recording studio**  A place to make music records.

## READ MORE

Huddleston, Emma. **Ed Sheeran.** Lake Elmo, MN: Focus Readers, 2020.

Rajczak Nelson, Kristen. **Ed Sheeran: Singer-Songwriter.** Enslow Publishing, 2019.

Whitaker, Chelsea. **Ed Sheeran.** Mason Crest, 2022.

## ON THE WEB

**All Music**
https://www.allmusic.com/artist/ed-sheeran-mn0002639628

**Official Website of Ed Sheeran**
https://www.edsheeran.com/


## INDEX



### About the Author

Jill Sherman writes books about pop stars, baby animals, and robots. She loves that writing allows her to research and learn about new topics. In addition to writing books, Jill sews her own clothes, creates crossword puzzles, and codes in JavaScript.

She listened to all of Ed Sheeran's music while writing this book.